KILLER NATURE!

# Big Cats

## Lynn Huggins-Cooper

**W**

FRANKLIN WATTS

LONDON • SYDNEY

First published in 2005
by Franklin Watts

Copyright © Franklin Watts 2005

Franklin Watts
338 Euston Road
London NW1 3BH

Franklin Watts Australia
Hachette Children's Books
Level 17/207 Kent Street
Sydney, NSW 2000

**Editor:** Jennifer Schofield
**Jacket designer:** Peter Scoulding
**Designer:** Jay Young
**Picture researcher:** Diana Morris

**Acknowledgements:**
Bios/Still Pictures: 1, 6. Alan & Sandy Carey/Still Pictures: front cover r, 7.
C. Dani & I. Jeske/Still Pictures: 28. M & C Denis-Huot/Still Pictures: 5t, 12,
17t, 17b, 24, 26-27b, 27t. M. Gunther/Still Pictures: 25. Martin Harvey/Still
Pictures: front cover bl, 11, 13, 14, 16. Klein/Hubert/Still Pictures: 18, 21, 29.
Klein/Still Pictures: 19, 23. S.J. Krasemann/Still Pictures: 20. Joe McDonald/
Corbis: 8. Fritz Polking/Still Pictures: 10t, 10b, 15. Jany Sauvanet/NHPA: 22.
Satyendra K Tiwari/OSF: 9. Hans Tomashoff/Still Pictures: front cover cl.
Tom Vezo/Still Pictures: 5b.

Every attempt has been made to clear copyright.
Should there be any inadvertent omission please
apply to the publisher for rectification.

A CIP catalogue record for this book
is available from the British Library.

**ISBN:** 978 0 7496 6094 9
**Dewey Classification:** 599.75

**Franklin Watts is a division of Hachette Children's Books.**

# Contents

# The biggest cats

Big cats may look furry and lovable
– just like pet cats. But the worst
your pet cat can do is catch a bird
or a mouse. The big cats found
in the wild are after much larger
prey – and that might mean that
you are on the menu!

## Man-eating beasts

Although most of the big cats are
thought of as man-eaters, they prefer
to avoid people altogether. They attack
people only when they feel threatened
and scared, or are injured.

Today, as new towns and farms are
built in the places where big cats hunt,
people are coming into contact more
often with these fierce creatures.
All around the world, there are stories
of killer cats that have attacked and
devoured livestock – and even people.

## Friend or foe?

Can you tell whether a big cat is a friend or foe? Is it safe to hike in the wilderness? Is that a dark shadow in the tree, or is it a deadly cougar waiting to pounce?

Read on to find out more about these predators. It just might save your life one day!

# Tigers in the snow

Siberian tigers are the largest member of the cat family. These striped heavy-weights are found in the wild far east of Russia, in India, southeast Asia, northern Korea and in northeast China.

## Vital statistics

Adult male Siberian tigers can easily weigh 300 kilograms. They can measure 2.8 metres from their nose to the tip of their tail and their tail alone can be over a metre long.

Females are smaller than males. They weigh up to 168 kilograms and can measure 2.4 metres in length.

There have been reports of tigers weighing an amazing 364 kilograms, but cats this size are very rare.

## Encounters with people

Occasionally, farmers shoot Siberian tigers to protect their livestock. There are many stories about tigers that have become 'man-eaters' but this is not common.

Usually, a tiger that hunts people is old or injured and finds hunting wild prey difficult. Tigers normally avoid people and will only attack if they feel threatened.

## How they kill

These stealthy killers hunt at night, hidden in the shadows of the long grass by their stripy camouflage.

Siberian tigers have good eyesight – their night vision is six times better than human night vision.

Tigers can run very fast for short distances. They can jump 3 metres in a single leap, making them very difficult to escape from! Tigers grip their victims with their front claws and then kill them with a deadly bite to the throat.

### Fact!

Tiger stripes are as unique as our fingerprints – no two tigers have exactly the same markings.

# More about tigers

## When tigers attack

The magician Roy Horn has worked with tigers for many years. In October 2003, he was injured when his seven-year-old royal white Siberian tiger, Montecore, attacked him. Horn told the tiger to lie down, but it would not.

Horn then tapped Montecore's nose with his microphone, but the tiger bit his arm. Next, Montecore grabbed Horn by the neck and knocked him down. Horn was badly injured and it took months for him to recover.

## Tiger cubs

Siberian tigers give birth to between two and four cubs at a time. The cubs are fed on their mother's milk until they are about two months old.

By the time the cubs are five months old, they are taught to hunt small animals. Tiger cubs live with their mother until they are about two years old.

## Survival

Thousands of Siberian tigers have been killed for their striped fur, teeth and claws. Although there are only 400–500 Siberian tigers left in the wild today, they are a conservation success story.

In the 1940s, Siberian tigers were facing extinction – there were only 24 Siberian tigers left. Once the tigers became a protected species, their numbers in the wild began to rise. There are also about 500 captive Siberian tigers in zoos and parks around the world.

## Fact!

Tigers can eat up to 45 kg of meat in one meal! After such a meal, they do not eat for several days.

# Lions on the prowl

Lions are often called the kings of the jungle, but they actually live in groups called prides on Africa's grassland plains.

## Vital statistics

After the Siberian tiger, the African lion is the second largest cat in the wild. Adult males can weigh up to 189 kilograms. The heaviest male on record weighed 272 kilograms.

Female African lions are leaner than males. They weigh up to 126 kilograms and are around 1.1 metres long.

### Fact!
Lions have facial markings called 'whisker spots'. These marks are like fingerprints – no two are the same.

## Encounters with people

Hunters from the Masai tribe, who herd cattle in east Africa, have lived with lions for centuries. When there are plenty of prey animals, such as gazelle, the lions are not a problem. But, if a drought or disease reduces the number of wild animals, lions are more likely to attack cattle – or even the herders.

## How they kill

In the lion pride, the females do most of the hunting. These powerful cats hunt in a 'tag team', where two or more lionesses take turns chasing prey until the prey is exhausted.

Sometimes the lionesses ambush animals, chasing their victims towards other lions that hide, waiting to pounce. Lionesses are strong enough to hunt large animals such as zebra, gazelle, wildebeest and even buffalo.

# More about lions

## Lion cubs

On average, lionesses give birth to three cubs in a litter. As they are unable to protect themselves, the cubs are hidden from other predators until they are about eight weeks old. Cubs are often cared for in groups or 'crèches' with other cubs from the same pride.

## When lions attack

Although African lions usually avoid humans, there have been some horrific attacks.

Based on a true story, the film *The Ghost and the Darkness* tells of two lions that killed 135 construction workers in just nine months.

In another terrible series of attacks in the 1920s, a single male lion killed 84 people in Ankole, Uganda.

## Fact!

Lions are incredibly lazy beasts – they can sleep for up to 21 hours a day.

## Survival

In 2004, there were about 20,000 lions in Africa. This may seem like a lot, but numbers are falling. In 1996, there were between 30,000 and 100,000 lions in the wild. Each year, at least 600 African lions are killed by hunters for their skin, claws and teeth.

# Tree-climbing leopards

Leopards are found in Africa and some parts of Asia, such as Sri Lanka. These beautiful, spotted big cats are fast runners and are especially skilled at climbing trees.

## Vital statistics

Leopards are small compared to lions and tigers. Males can weigh between 37.2 and 89.8 kilograms and measure 1.5 to 2.03 metres from nose to tail.

Female leopards are a lot smaller than the males, measuring between 1.22 and 1.5 metres in length.

### Fact!

Some leopards have such dark fur that their spots are hidden. They are called black panthers.

## Encounters with people

When they live near villages and farms, leopards attack domestic animals such as goats and pigs. This makes them a nuisance, and farmers shoot and trap them.

In India, leopard numbers have increased but the numbers of their wild prey animals have not. This has led to more leopard attacks on cattle and people.

## How they kill

Leopards are silent hunters. They stalk their prey, sneaking up to it until they are very close. Then they seize their victim around the neck and throat, holding on until the animal cannot breathe.

Leopards are good climbers, and may drag a large kill up a tree to avoid losing it to other carnivores. Sometimes they store their kills in trees to eat later.

# More about leopards

## Little leopards

Female leopards make a den in a hidden area, such as a cave or thick bushes. They give birth to a litter of two to four cubs in the den.

At about three months old, the cubs go with their mother on hunts. When the cubs are about a year old, they can hunt for themselves, but they stay with their mother for another year or so.

## When leopards attack

Although leopards are smaller than many of the other big cats, they are one of the most fearsome. A ferocious leopard, known as the 'Kahani man-eater', killed more than 200 people. In India, leopards have killed 37 people and injured 652 since 1995.

## The great escape

In 1997, a leopard escaped from a zoo in Mumbai, India. After attacking two elderly men, it ran into an empty house. It smashed crockery, ate a cooked meal and then fell asleep in the kitchen sink. It was shot with a tranquilliser dart and taken back to the zoo.

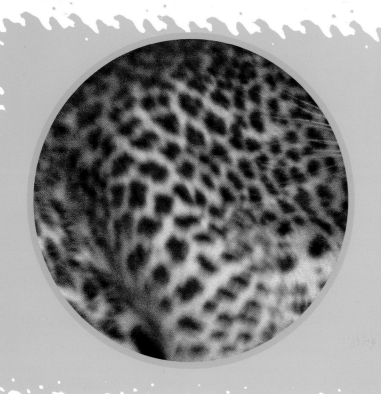

## Survival

For centuries, leopards have been hunted for their beautiful fur. In the 1960s, as many as 50,000 leopards were killed every year.

Hunting leopards is now illegal in most parts of the world. In many countries, leopards are listed as an endangered species. This is not just because of hunting, but also because their natural habitat is being destroyed.

# Deadly cougars

Cougars, or mountain lions, are found across the Americas from Canada to Chile. They live in mountains, forests, deserts and grassland areas.

These fierce cats are often seen in Western films attacking livestock – and even cowboys. But do they deserve their bad reputation?

## Vital statistics

Male cougars are larger than females and can weigh up to 120 kilograms. Females are a lot lighter, at about 64 kilograms. From nose to tail, males measure about 2.5 metres and females up to 2 metres.

## Encounters with people

As more people build houses in areas where cougars live, and increasingly spend time trekking in wilderness areas, there are more meetings between these big cats and people.

Cougars are now fairly common in the suburbs of California. Some have been seen as far east as Kansas City, Missouri, where several have been hit by cars.

## How they kill

These cats stalk their prey until they are about 15 metres away. When they are close enough, they dash the last few metres, leaping onto the animal's back and breaking its neck with a powerful, deadly bite. Sometimes cougars hide their kill to keep it safe from other animals.

### Fact!

The female cougar has a strange, eerie cry that sounds like a human scream.

# More about cougars

## Survival

For many years, cougars were hunted for money and their numbers fell dramatically. In the 1960s, there were only 6,500 cougars in the wild. However, today there are over 20,000 cougars. This is because only a set number of cougars can be hunted each year.

## Cougar kittens

Cougars may have from one to six kittens, but on average there are three to four kittens in a litter.

The kittens are spotty when they are born, but they lose their spots after a few months. Like many animals, cougars are born with closed eyes but they open after about ten days.

At first the kittens drink their mother's milk, but they are fully weaned onto meat after about 40 days. Cougars stay with their mother for up to two years.

## Real-life story

In 1986, Justin Mellon, aged 6, was grabbed by a cougar in Caspers Regional Park, California. The cat took Justin's head in its mouth and tried to drag him away. The boy's father attacked the cougar with a knife and luckily it ran away. Justin needed 100 stitches to close his bite wounds.

## When cougars attack

Cougars would prefer to avoid people, but about four humans are killed by these dangerous cats each year. When hiking in wilderness areas, it is important to be on your guard in case cougars mistake you for a prey animal. In British Columbia, Canada, signs are posted on hiking trails warning walkers to be careful.

# Jaguars on the hunt

Jaguars are found in many regions of the Americas, from the southwestern United States to Argentina, as far south as Patagonia.

Their habitat ranges from the South American grassy plains, to deserts in Mexico and the USA. They are also found in the Amazon jungle.

## Fact!
Most jaguars are golden with black spots – but some are pitch-black.

## Vital statistics

Jaguars may look like leopards but they are more sturdily built and heavier. Males usually weigh between 56 and 113 kilograms and females between 40 and 90 kilograms.

Jaguars can measure between 1.2 and 1.8 metres long. Interestingly, their size changes from place to place. Jaguars that live in open country tend to be larger than those living in the jungle.

## What's for dinner?

Jaguars are not afraid of killing large animals. They hunt deer, peccaries (wild pigs) and even fierce caimans (crocodiles) while they bask beside water. In the Amazon rainforest, jaguars also eat fish, frogs and turtles.

## How they kill

These cunning cats do not stalk or chase prey. Instead, jaguars hide and ambush unsuspecting victims as they pass by. They kill large animals by biting through the skull between the ears.

## Encounters with people

Jaguars are very territorial cats. When their forest habitats are cleared for farming, jaguars often kill the domestic animals that they find there.

There are many stories about people being followed through the jungle by jaguars. As the jaguars do not usually attack people, it is thought that they are not stalking them as prey. Instead, they are making sure the people leave their territory.

# More about jaguars

## Jaguar cubs

Each year, female jaguars give birth to a litter of one to four cubs in a den made in thorny undergrowth or under the roots of trees.

The cubs learn to hunt at about three to six months old. Like many of the big cats, they stay with their mother for about two years.

## When jaguars attack

Although the Yanomami tribe calls the jaguar the 'eater of souls', jaguars rarely attack humans in the wild.

However, in 2002, three jaguars attacked and killed a zookeeper after she entered their cage. Officials at the Vienna zoo said that the jaguars had burst into the cage through a hatch that had not been locked.

## Tunnelling out

In 1998, two jaguars tunnelled out of their enclosure at a zoo near Poitiers in France. One of the big cats headed straight for a group of people and turned on a four-year-old boy, Gregoire Lucazeau. The little boy was mauled to death by the 100-kilogram, cat and his father was badly injured as he tried to save his son.

## Survival

There are an about 15,000 jaguars left in the wild. In the 1960s, 18,000 jaguars were killed each year for their fur. Today, although jaguars are protected, they are still hunted and killed by poachers for their fur.

# Super-quick cheetahs

Instead of using skill to hunt, cheetahs rely on their incredible speed. These sleek cats are the world's fastest land animals. They can cover 7 to 8 metres in a single stride and may take four strides in one second.

## Vital statistics

Cheetahs need to be streamlined and light to run at speeds of up to 95 kph. They are much lighter than other big cats and weigh between 34 and 54 kilograms. Male cheetahs are slightly larger than the females. They measure 67 to 94 centimetres from foot to shoulder, and 1.9 to 2.3 metres from nose to tail.

## How they kill

A cheetah finds a high place, such as a tree stump, from which to watch for prey. It moves closer to the prey, to within 50 metres, before it dashes in for the kill.

The cheetah knocks its victim down with the powerful force of its charge. The animal is then grabbed by the neck and strangled to death.

## Young cheetahs

Cheetahs have three to five cubs in a litter. For the first few weeks, the mother moves the cubs every few days to avoid other predators.

Cheetah cubs begin to follow their mother around at six weeks. When they are about six months old, they are weaned and their mother begins to teach them to hunt.

# Fearsome lynx

With their short tails and tufted ears, Canadian lynx look quite different from the other big cats.

They are found not only in Canada, but also in western Montana, parts of Idaho, and Washington State, USA.

## Survival

Canadian lynx have been killed for their fur since the 1600s. However, poachers are not their biggest problem.

The numbers of the smaller animals that lynx prey on, such as hares and voles, have dropped because their habitat has been destroyed. When there are fewer prey animals, there is less food for the lynx. As a result, the Canadian lynx population drops.

## Vital statistics

Canadian lynx are only about twice the size of pet cats. They grow to a length of about 1.3 metres and can weigh up to 45 kilograms.

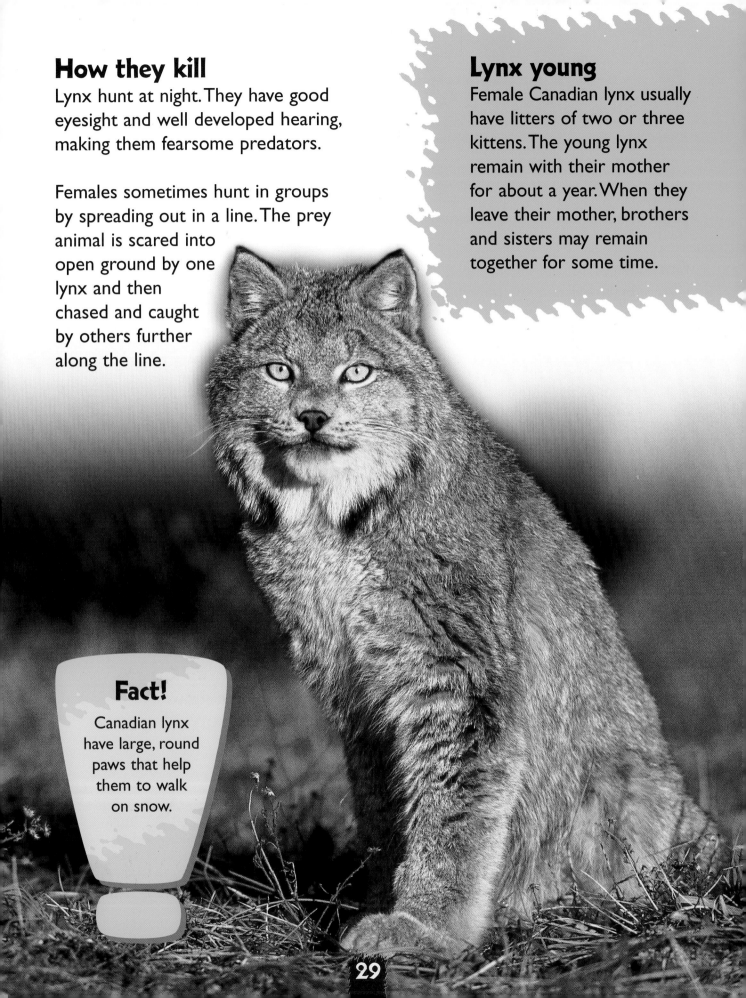

## How they kill

Lynx hunt at night. They have good eyesight and well developed hearing, making them fearsome predators.

Females sometimes hunt in groups by spreading out in a line. The prey animal is scared into open ground by one lynx and then chased and caught by others further along the line.

## Lynx young

Female Canadian lynx usually have litters of two or three kittens. The young lynx remain with their mother for about a year. When they leave their mother, brothers and sisters may remain together for some time.

### Fact!

Canadian lynx have large, round paws that help them to walk on snow.

# Key words

**Ambush**
A surprise attack from a hidden place.

**Camouflage**
The special colours or markings found on plants and animals that help them to remain hidden.

**Captive**
The animals that are kept in zoos or special conservation enclosures.

**Carnivores**
The animals that eat only meat.

**Conservation**
Keeping the natural environment in a good state. For example, protecting animals and their habitats.

**Den**
A home or hiding place of a wild animal.

**Endangered species**
A group of living things in danger of dying out completely.

**Extinction**
When a group of living things dies out completely, we say it is extinct.

**Habitat**
The place where particular plants and animals live.

**Horn, Roy (1944–)**
One of the magicians of the Siegfried and Roy show. For the last 30 years, big cats have featured in their acts.

**Litter**
A number of young animals born at the same time to the same parent.

**Livestock**
The animals, such as cows and sheep, that are farmed by people.

**Mammal**
An animal with fur or hair which feeds its young with its own milk.

**Night vision**
A person's or animal's ability to see at night or in the dark.

**Predators**
The animals that hunt other animals.

**Prey**
The animals hunted by other animals for food.

## Pride
A group of lions that live together.

## Protected species
A group of animals protected by laws to ensure its survival.

## Streamlined
When an animal has a smooth shape to help it move more easily through the air or water.

## Territorial
Describes an animal that guards its home. Many animals mark their territory with urine.

## Tranquilliser dart
A special kind of dart that is shot into an animal to make it fall asleep.

## Weaned
When a young mammal stops drinking its mother's milk and eats other food, such as meat.

## Western films
The films about the people of western America in the late 19th and early 20th centuries.

## Yanomami
The tribe of native Americans that lives in the rainforests of Venezuela and northern Brazil.

# Weblinks

**www.worldwildlife.org**
Loads of fun-filled games, facts and information on the World Wildlife Fund (WWF) charity.

**www.bigcatrescue. org**
Free games, pictures, screensavers, and information on wildlife.

**www.kidskonnect.com/Animals/ZooLinks.html**
Access weblinks for zoos from all over the world.

**www.kidsplanet.org/**
Fact files, games and quizzes about many of the big cats.

**www.enchantedlearning.com/Home.html**
Lots of information on all the big cats, things to make and pictures to download and colour.

**www.zooquarium.com.au**
Wonderful photographs of wild cats, animated tours and information.

**Note to parents:**
Every effort has been made by the publishers to ensure that the websites in this book are suitable for children, that they are of the highest educational value, and that they contain no inappropriate or offensive material. However, due to the nature of the Internet, it is impossible to guarantee that the contents of these sites will not be altered. We strongly advise that Internet access is supervised by a responsible adult.

# Index